The Loving Father

Parables of Jesus in Cartoon
Words by Meryl Doney
Pictures by Graham Round

When Jesus wanted to teach his friends
something important he used to say:
'I'll tell you a story. Listen very hard
and you will understand it.'
The Loving Father is one of the
stories Jesus told.

Winston Windows

Jesus had many friends who were not good people. He loved them all. But the good people did not like this.

'How can he love these bad people?' they said to themselves. 'God only loves good people.'

Jesus heard them. 'God loves everyone,' he said. 'He wants to forgive people who have been bad. He can help them to be good.'

His friends said, 'Tell us what God is like.'

So Jesus told them this story.

Once upon a time, there was a rich man who had two sons.

He promised to give his money to his sons when he died.

The elder son was good. He said, 'I'll stay at home to help, father.'

But the younger son did not want to help his father.

'Please give me my share of the money now,' he said. 'I want to go away and enjoy myself.'

So he took his money, and left home. His father was very sad.

The younger son went off to the big city. He had a wonderful time.

He bought a grand house and beautiful clothes and a horse to ride.

He had lots of friends. He invited them to parties at his house.

Soon all his money was gone.

So he sold his house, his horse and even his beautiful clothes.

His friends all left him. Before long he had no food left to eat.

He had to take a job looking after pigs. He was so hungry he even ate their food.

Then he remembered his father and his home.

'I have done all the wrong things,' he said to himself. 'Will my father forgive me?'

'I will go home,' he decided. 'Perhaps he will let me be a servant.'

So he set off on the long journey home. He walked all the way.

At last, he saw his home. There was someone outside . . .

It was his father. He ran to meet his son because he was so glad to see him. He still loved him very much.

'Father I have been very wrong,' said the son. 'Will you forgive me?'

'Yes,' said his father. 'I have waited every day for you to come home.'

'Bring him new clothes, and a ring,' he called. 'Get ready for a party!'

'My son is sorry for all he has done. I have forgiven him. I am so happy.'

They had a wonderful party. Everyone danced and sang for joy.

'God is like that father,' said Jesus.
'He wants people to come and say they are sorry for being bad. Then he will forgive them and help them to be good. When that happens, he is very happy, just like the father in my story.'

You can find this story in your Bible:
Luke 15:11-32